How I Got Over:

Testimonies of God's Amazing Grace

Compiled by Crystal Jones

Authors: Jake Allen, Keila Allen, Marie Arias, Domini Baldwin, Nickerson Bonhomme, Orlanda Bonhomme, Sherri Bryant, Cleaver Davis, Pamela Gary, Karen Grier, Keith Grier, Crystal Jones, Oscar Jones, Rochelle Smith, Claudia Thomas, LaShara White, Aries Winans, Kim Winans-Edwards, Tony Winans,

How I Got Over:

Testimonies of God's Amazing Grace

published by
Destiny House Publishing, LLC.
P.O. Box 19774
Detroit, MI 48219

inquiry@destinyhousepublishing.com

www.destinyhousepublishing.com

404.993.0830

Cover by Kingdom Graphic Designs

Printed in the United States

ISBN: 978-1-936867-99-8

Acknowledgments:

Thank you to the Lord of Hosts, our Kind King and Righteous Redeemer who gifted us these life-changing testimonies. We are forever grateful. We pray that these stories will impact the lives of many for your glory.

❖

Thanks to all of the authors who participated in this project. It was hard work. Thank you for your transparency, love for God and the courage to share what God has done on your behalf.

❖

Special thanks to Greater Works Family Ministries, The Love Culture, and Alive International Ministries.

❖

Thank you to Kingdom Graphic Designs and Mrs. Aries Winans for your creative and artistic design of our cover. We appreciate you.

Table of Contents

Introduction

Life be life-ing! It's slang for life is filled with challenges, trials, and just stuff to navigate. Anyone with a pulse knows, it can be rough out here in these streets. Life is full of ups and downs, bumps and jolts. None of us our immune, we all experience its turbulence. So how do we get through life when it feels that all is going awry? The answer is simple and complex. We must look to the one true God, the One who laid His life down for us. Jesus has a plan for each of us. He will throw us a lifeline. We simply have to trust Him enough to grab it.

Welcome to *How I Got Over: Testimonies of God's Amazing Grace.* This book is a kaleidoscope of stories from ordinary people who testify about God's extraordinary power. This collective of authors are overcomers beckoning you on their journey. You will find stories that will make you smile, shed a tear or even provoke you to deep thought. It is our hope that you will find some answers or encouragement for your own trek.

These story tellers share various testimonies from overcoming cancer, healing a broken marriage, breaking addictions, holding on to life when they should've been dead, etc. Their tales remind us that God is always at work even when we least expect it. Somehow He shows up in our stories as the fourth man in the fire. We are not consumed. The Lord commands a great turnaround. What the devil meant to destroy us, God uses it for our good.

Yes, miracles, signs, and wonders are still available today. God's power is just as fervent as it has always been. It doesn't fizzle or decline over time. The same power that raised Jesus from the dead is at work inside of those who love Him.

But let me encourage you, God loves you completely, regardless of whether you love him back. Romans 5:8 (NKJV) reminds us, "But God demonstrates His own love toward us, in that while we were still sinners, Christ died for us." Lean into His love. He will surprise you.

There are two responses we should have to God's amazing grace and love. The first is gratitude. As a result of the gratitude, it should prompt us to share our testimony.

Introduction

Psalm 105:1 reads Oh give thanks to the LORD, call upon His name; **Make known His deeds among the peoples**.

In other words, tell someone. As God brings you out of whatever pit that you find yourself, be appreciative and bold enough to share your own triumphs. When Jesus healed the 10 lepers, only one returned to thank Him. Remember to say thank you. Then share what God has done for you. It's how we give Him glory.

This compilation is not meant to be read in any specific order. Read by topics or by chapters. Feel free to share these stories with others to encourage them in their own journey.

So, find a cozy spot, maybe a cup of tea, hot chocolate, or lemonade. and dive in. Because in a world that can sometimes feel overwhelming, these stories are like a beacon of light, reminding us that we're never alone — and that, with God's grace on our side there's nothing we can't overcome.

It is our prayer that you will be encouraged and fired up with hope to get over the mountains you face. May your soul look back and declare, "I know how I got over! Thank you, Lord for your incredible grace".

My mouth shall tell of Your righteousness And Your salvation all the day, For I do not know their limits. [16] I will go in the strength of the Lord God; I will make mention of Your righteousness, of Yours only. [17] O God, You have taught me from my youth; And to this day I declare Your wondrous works. -Psalm 71:15-17

DELIVERANCE FROM SEXUAL IMMORALITY

Introduction

Church Girl Gone Wild

Keila Allen, Forest Park, GA

The melody of the song, "Somebody Prayed for Me" (by Dorthy Norwood and Alvin Darling) plays in my mind as I take this moment to share my salvation journey. I hear these words over and over again ... somebody prayed for me, they had me on their mind, took some time to pray for me, I'm so glad they prayed, I'm so glad they prayed, I'm so glad they prayed for me.

Most of my life from age five to present consisted of being raised and trained in a church setting. I had the opportunity to attend church with my family. This included my parents, grandparents, aunts, uncles, cousins, etc. Going to church was like going to a big family dinner every Sunday with lots of music and love. There was a pattern, a routine, to follow... Sunday School, regular service, dinner in the fellowship hall, and then the second service. We woke up around 9 a.m. and came home around 5 or p.m. Does this sound like a work schedule to you? Yep, it truly was, it was a very long day, and it was work.

Fast forward thirteen years later, my life felt as though it swiftly progressed, and I was an adult having to make many decisions in life on my own. At this time, I was about 18 years old. I went to college two weeks after high school. My grades weren't up to par, so I had to complete a summer program to become eligible to register for school in the Fall.

I went from living in my parents' home to living on campus at the University. I was a church girl gone wild. Yep, that's exactly what happened from middle school leading into college. I was sneaky and very loose. I didn't honor God with my body; I was very promiscuous. I tried many things but never went too far with anything. I tried smoking, but didn't like it. I tried drinking, but didn't want to be drunk. I joined a sorority, but didn't stay long. I dibbled and dabbled in sin and didn't take God's word seriously. All the years of being in church and hearing God's word didn't change my heart posture or behavior. I had the word in my head, but it hadn't changed my heart. What?!?

Can you believe this? Yep. The problem was that I became comfortable with hearing the word over the years, taking God's grace for granted and not actually applying His word to my life.

Rules without relationship is just religion. I was lacking a real loving relationship with God.

It gets better…In my early twenties, I grew tired of my sinful and religious lifestyle and desired something more from God. I started attending Bible studies on the college campus and joined the Oakland University Gospel Choir.

God had a plan. The Lord met me at every rehearsal. Over the course of time, my heart grew closer to the Lord by being a part of this choir. The power of the Lord met us at every rehearsal and every engagement. The encounters that I had with the Lord grew to so many that I could no longer count.

This is the initial time in my life where I was significantly impacted by the Lord. I repented to God, and began a new journey. I accepted Jesus as my personal Lord and Savior. I changed by behavior. My words started to match my actions. My heart wanted God. My choices mattered this time. I didn't want to hurt God. This time was different, and I knew that I wasn't turning back.

As more songs continue to play in my mind while I'm telling my story, I'm reminded of how some of those songs became attached to my new pattern of living. My mind's made up, no turning back, yes I'm happy, 'cause I'm on the right track. Some of the gospel songs from back in the day, really hit differently, when you sing them. The words carry so much power. The Bible states that words are spirit and life. Although, I didn't practice applying God's word earlier in my life, I'm so grateful that I was there to hear the spoken word over and over again. Eventually, those words became life to me and led me back to God.

If you are reading this right now, I want to encourage you in this moment. If you believe that this story resonates with where you are in your walk with God, don't hesitate to repent right now. As long as there is breath in your body, there is time to make things right with the Lord. The Lord wants your whole heart. Choose to live for Him right now where you are. Pray this prayer with me: Heavenly Father I am here with you and I need you. I desire a true and intimate relationship with you. I repent of my sins. Your word says in 1 John 1:9 that if I confess my sins, you are faithful and just to forgive me from my sins and to cleanse me from all unrighteousness. Give me a clean heart and renew the right spirit within me. I want to live for you. Help me to choose your ways every day in Jesus Name, Amen.

The melody returns…I'm so glad they prayed, I'm so glad they prayed, I'm so glad they prayed for me!

Saying Yes

Kim Winans, East Pointe, MI

It all started with my brother lusting after a woman he met at the gas station. He asked her out. They ended up talking for about a week. The young lady asked if he would go to church with her and her friend. He agreed.

My brother was living with me at the time, so they all agreed to meet at my house. They met up several times after that day. During one of their visits, the two young ladies and one of my brothers sat in the living room to wait for my other brother to come to the house. While they waited, the young ladies began talking about the goodness of God.

I was about 26 years old. Although the young lady was only 15 years old, the words she spoke really got my attention. She was really breaking through to me. Just as she was getting ready to tell be about becoming a believer, we received a phone call that my brother had just been shot.

My newborn baby was lying next to me on the couch, so I couldn't leave to go see my brother. All I could do was cry.

The young lady told me not to worry and she began to pray for me. Her prayer penetrated my heart. As I continued to listen, I felt a peace blanket over me that I didn't understand, and I began to relax. I couldn't figure out why I didn't feel afraid or upset anymore. I didn't know what was happening. She then said, "God said he's gonna be OK. He's not going to die." I believed her.

When my brother arrived at the hospital, he called me to say he was in the EMS, and he was going to be okay. He said the bullet only really grazed him. But I already knew he was going to be ok because I believed what the young lady said God told her after she prayed for me.

After the phone call ended, she said that she wanted to lead me through the sinner's prayer and explained that I could repent of my sins and accept Jesus as my Lord and Savior. I said, "Yes!" She had me repeat the prayer after her. I accepted Jesus and I believed with my whole heart and to this day my mindset is still right there because I know God is real!

Once the prayer ended, I asked, "What now"? She said, that's it! I started going to church with her. Newly saved, I was excited to share the word of God with others.

Shortly after I gave my life to Christ, I met this pretty handsome guy. He and I would go to church together. We became boyfriend and girlfriend pretty quickly as we were really falling for each other.

At church, the messages the pastor preached were like arrows to my heart. I really wanted to live right. One day, the pastor preached against fornication and my heart sunk, because my boyfriend and I were sleeping together at that time. As he continued to preach, I prayed silently in my heart and asked God what did I need to do because I loved my boyfriend; but I loved God more. I was beginning to understand that my choices were not pleasing to God.

I learned that fornication and smoking were NOT things that glorified the Lord, so I didn't want to do them anymore. People began to make fun of me and say that I was boring. As if sin was the only way to have fun. I just knew in my heart that God was leading me in a different direction.

During another Sunday service, the word came forth about living together (shacking up). I surrendered to the word. I told my boyfriend that he had to move out and that we couldn't sleep together anymore. He said that he understood because his grandparents were also pastors. When he was younger, they taught him that as well.

Shortly thereafter, he got into trouble and went to jail. We had only been together for about 2 ½ months. He was sentenced to 90 days. In my heart, I began to think maybe we should break up because he was going to spend more time in jail than he had been with me. I told him we aren't married, and I didn't want to live in violation of God's word.

This was a difficult time for me because I loved him, and I loved how well he treated me. While he was in prison, he spoke to his grandmother quite a bit and she ministered the word of God to him. He began to write me letters and tell me how I was the queen of his heart and he was still trying to live right. He told me how he was changing for the better. I talked about going to church and how there was such a spirit of joy there and that we should go together. I loved what was happening in my heart and I didn't want it to end. God was giving me a peace that I had never known. Although I loved my boyfriend, I needed him to know about my deepened love for God. He knew that I was different, and he loved the change in me, too.

When he was released, he went home to his cousin's house. Shortly after, he came to visit me. What I didn't know was that he went to his grandmother's house to get his mother's wedding band that she had been holding for him. He came to me, got down on one knee and asked me to marry him. Of course, I said, "Yes!"

As we fell deeper in love with the word, I watched our relationship thrive. In our apartment complex where we lived, there was a small community of men, at least 4 brothers from the church, met regularly. My boyfriend went to one of their meetings and really enjoyed it. The men poured into him, and he grew in his faith. We began going to church together. Two people, trying to live right for Jesus.

My boyfriend and I married that same year in December. Although we had only been together for some months, I felt like I had known him for years. He was very good to me. By this time, I was 29 years old.

We had become serious about our walk with Christ. I placed a sign on my front door that read, 'No smoking, drinking, or cursing allowed". I believed God was trying to strip me so He could build me. I wanted no temptations. He was taking everything away so he could build me to be the woman He wanted me to be. I didn't know it at that time but that's exactly what He was doing in me.

I later learned that my brother and sister were upset with me because they felt like I was making my kids' lives boring because we went to church so often. They tried to have protective services take my kids from me. I was really upset with them. I cried out to God to work the situation out for us so they wouldn't take our kids. My family felt we were in a cult because we were in church 3 days a week. My heart was to do what was best for my children and not be moved by their opinions. God said yes to my petition. And we did not lose our children.

My husband and I had many challenges over the years. But God brought us through every single one. In 2010 we celebrated 20 years of marriage. Sadly, he passed just 2 months after that. My husband left this earth with his faith firmly intact. To God be the glory! God had his hand on us the whole time. I am so glad that I said Yes to God. I have no regrets. I thank Him for the journey.

Fighting Temptations

Rochelle Smith, Detroit, MI

I was raised by a single mom, who had five children by five different fathers. Most of our fathers were pretty absent, except for my last sibling. My mother married his father, and their marriage lasted for several years until she passed.

In those years, I lived an average African American childhood. My mom was on welfare. My grandmother was the one who raised me and my siblings. My mother did the best she could in my younger years. But she drank a lot and my dad was what you would call *a rolling stone*. He had his share of women. My mother moved out and left me and my siblings to raise ourselves. You can imagine how we lived. One by one, my siblings left until I was the only one living alone at 12 years old. I eventually went to live with my grandmother.

My siblings and I had our share of fights with neighborhood families, and school cliques. A lot of fights were brought to our doorsteps. There were shoot outs and cocktails thrown. It was only by God's grace that we were not harmed.

I had some great years as a child and some not-so-great years. My upbringing introduced me to a lot of things as a teenager. I skipped school a lot. I started partying and hanging out at clubs and cabarets at the age of 12 with my older siblings, friends, and family. I started drinking at the age of 14 and smoking marijuana at the age of 17. We missed school a lot.

This life led to regular nights of partying, where I would be drunk and high, hanging out with friends, at house parties, motorcycle clubs, night clubs, drugs houses and dance parties where my friends would dance for men. I thought I was a little too good for that until I got into a financial hardship. I secretly started calling strip clubs to get information about how I could become a dancer. Thanks to God I didn't have the courage to show up.

I was a virgin until I was 17 years old. Where I'm from - that was something to celebrate. I had two long-lasting on and off relationships, one short relationship and two one-nightstands. I wanted to be like my friends, so I had the one-night stands, but I quickly found out that I didn't like it. It just wasn't me.

I have had my share of disappointments in those longer lasting relationships, but the one that I was in prior to getting saved was the toughest one. It would bring me to the altar as if I was sacrificing a bull to rid myself from the guilt of sinning, but unfortunately I would return right to it.

Towards the end of that relationship, I knew that the Lord was working with me. The Holy Spirit would be dealing with me even in the midst of the act. I would tell the person I was with that this was *not* God's will for me and what we're doing is not good. But I gave in even as I cried. I was convicted of my sin. The Lord was drawing me closer to him, and I knew it.

While I was in the club with friends. I was looking around wondering why I was there. Something was changing in me. I would smoke weed and cigars, and it would have a nasty taste in my mouth. Drinking was no longer pleasing to me. My language began to change. It was like the Lord was washing me clean, all at once.

But the relationship I was in was the hardest thing to pull away from. It was because of lust. It wasn't that he was the person for me. The Lord would talk to me, and I would be in the mirror, talking back to him, telling him how hard it would be to not fornicate. I told him that he didn't understand, and that Jesus was perfect, and I could never stop what I was doing.

I remember the day when I invited my guy friend over. I knew that this would be the last day. It was so strong in my heart when he arrived and when he left that was it. I felt relieved knowing that this relationship was finally over, and I wanted to live my life for God. I watched him walk to his car and I smiled and said it's over.

From that point, February 27, 2003, I have been free of marijuana, drinking, cursing, living in a deceitful life, manipulating, fornication, etc. I finished high school and graduated from college and received my master's degree in business administration.

To God be the glory. I continue to die daily, but there is no other life that I would prefer than this life in Christ Jesus.

Free Indeed!

Jake Allen, Forest Park, GA

I had a heart full of lust and sexual perversion. Sexual perversion was the anchor that held me captive to pornography and womanizing. I went from woman to woman looking for fulfillment, only to come up empty.

I remember being introduced to pornography by my older cousin at 13 years old. At the time, I didn't know that watching it was harmful, so it became a normal part of my life. As I grew older, I knew it wasn't good. For many years. I found myself entangled in a cycle of unhealthy thoughts and behaviors. It seemed I would never escape.

What began as curiosity in my teenage years quickly morphed into an obsession that consumed my mind and distorted my understanding of relationships and intimacy. I felt trapped in a web of shame and guilt, believing that I could never be free from the darkness of porn and secrecy.

By the time I graduated from high school, I was already a dad. My daughter was born the December before high school graduation. I was gambling, drinking, smoking marijuana and doing whatever I wanted. I would often here about all the potential I had but my decisions where sending me down a road I would regret later on. My life was spiraling out of control. My mother was worried. She decided that it was best if I moved to Detroit to live with my father.

I remember going to my parents' church and being challenged to surrender my life to God. I felt it was time that I dedicated my life to the Lord. So I did that summer of 2000. This was in opposition to my core belief that a woman was all that I needed. Even though, I was raised in the church, I had never made a *real* commitment to serving God.

I began fellowshipping with a group of brothers that shared my struggles and became vulnerable and transparent with them. I discovered that many of my behaviors were linked to deeper issues, such as low self-esteem and a lack of healthy boundaries. I cried out to God often to heal these wounds and give me a true encounter with Him. My faith in Jesus was the source of my hope to get true deliverance of this madness I had experience all these years.

My commitment to God and transformation weren't easy. but I was finally honest with myself and made the hard choices to get it right. I repented of my sins and got saved for real. I prayed and meditated on the word of God often. I also sought personal counseling and guidance. I will never forget the challenge that I received from my pastors, "Give God one total year of all of you." Boy was this really a BIG DEAL! The first commitment that I made to myself and God was the decision to go through a total detachment of all things that I thought I needed to bring satisfaction. My relationship with Jesus and support team became a cornerstone of my recovery.

The next decision that I made was to break off my relationship with my girlfriend. This was a also a huge decision. I also stopped smoking and made a big change in the kind of music that I listened to. It was my goal to eliminate as many distractions as possible. My heart solely desired to bring God glory!

My commitment to God was my priority and I didn't want to let anything replace that. During this time of my life the Lord would give me dreams and visions often. I could hear His voice clearer. I spent countless hours in worship and prayer. Slowly, but surely, the grip of sexual perversion loosened its hold on me. It is a daily fight against the enemy, but I am committed to the fight.

Today, I stand thankful to the Lord for the progress I've made. I still face challenges, but I approach them with the help of the Holy Spirit. I have learned to keep my mind stayed on Christ and not to underestimate the power of meditating on God's word when sexual temptation arises. My journey is ongoing, but I am committed to living a holy life of authenticity and integrity.

To anyone who might be struggling with sexual perversion, I want to say; there is hope in Christ Jesus. Change is possible and you are not alone. Healing is a journey, not a destination. As you flee sexual immorality, resist the devil, and submit to God your future will get brighter and brighter.

Today, I am married with 5 children. My wife and I work together in ministry. I am feeding God's people by teaching and preaching the word. God is so good. He honors his word and is forever faithful to His promises. I often reflect on those times and now fully understand how important my decision to be free was. It was that decision that led me to where I am today. It was because He chose me and I chose him back. I see the fruit of His love and mercy upon me daily. I thank God He called me, and I answered.

FINANCIAL
MIRACLES

Raise Your Faith

Crystal Jones, Coconut Creek, FL

I was working for a Christian school. Every year, the employees were given raises. This particular year, employees were given a notice that because of financial shortfalls, no raises would be given out. We were disappointed to say the least. But I heard the Lord tell me to go to the president of the school and ask her for a raise. I was hesitant because we had all just received the same memo. I asked, "God is this you?" I couldn't shake it. I felt like it was the Lord.

So I did as I was instructed. The president of the school told me in no uncertain terms, that *no one* was getting a raise. So she would not be able to honor my request. She was nice about it, but firm. I said okay and went back to work. I told the Lord, "I did what you asked". After that, I didn't think any more about it.

Two weeks later, when I got paid, I opened my check. To my surprise, I had been given a significant increase. It was larger than our normal increase. I rejoiced. Only God can do that. To God be all the glory!

Lost and Found

Oscar Jones, Detroit, MI

I was driving down the street when I realized I had lost my payroll check. My heart was beating quickly. No one wants to lose 2 weeks' worth of income. My large family really needed that money.

I was driving down Northwestern Highway in Southfield, Michigan. Anxious, I prayed desperately for the Lord to help me find it. I stopped at a red light on the service drive. The wind had picked up a piece of paper. It flew right next to my car. I looked down on the ground to realize it was actually my payroll check that was blowing down the street. It landed right next to my car. There is no question about it, God gave me my check back supernaturally. It was really a miracle!

FORGIVENESS

The Good Father

Orlanda Bonhomme, Hollywood, FL

I grew up in church. My mom was a Christian and my dad went to church occasionally, but I had never really seen him devote his life to Christ like my mom.

My parents had 4 children. I was the only girl. My mom raised us in church and taught us about God. My mom's life was a walking testimony of how the power of God moved in her life and those she crossed paths with.

As a child, I've always felt different and never really felt understood. I grew up having lots of friends and making great connections but always felt alone and separated from others. There was always the feeling that I didn't belong. I spent most of my life in church only understanding the God that my mom served was a scary God and If I didn't do what he said I was going to hell. That gave me so much fear as a child. I didn't want to make God angry, but nobody ever really explained to me the depth of God's love for me. So, I lived a life of fear, learning to pray over my food, learned a couple of scriptures, I had a fear of my natural dad and God.

My dad was very tough on me. Even though he disciplined us for misbehaving, a lot of times it was for silly things. I would consider it more abuse than anything. As I continued to grow older, I grew more fearful of my dad and scared to make any type of mistake. I was a child that didn't talk a lot because of the way my dad treated me. He made life hard and almost impossible to live. I thought about running away plenty of times. I frequently wondered to myself if I would ever make it to 18 years old.

My dad would go to Haiti from time to time. This would give me an opportunity to breathe. I realized as an adult he was probably reflecting what he saw growing up.

Usually, I've heard the relationship that dad and a daughter had was beautiful. My story was the opposite. At the age of 15 years old I went to church with a friend. That day it was raining so bad, they were unable to take me home. I told my friend and her aunt that I was going to get in trouble because of getting home so late. I knew my dad was not going to tolerate me coming home so late. By the time I made it home it was probably 7:00 pm or 8:00 pm. When I made it home my friend's aunt tried to explain to my dad the situation, but he just closed the door in her face. That day was one of the worse days of my life. I was never given an opportunity to explain myself. My dad physically hit me. I said some words that were not appropriate. I felt like nothing I did was ever good enough for my dad. That night I got kicked out of the house and had to live with my godmother. At 15 years old I felt lost, hurt, defeated, unloved, without protection and that's when men took advantage of me. It felt like I was living a nightmare.

In those times in my life, I never questioned God, but I cried a lot. I was supposed to be a child, but I was having to grow up so fast, it didn't seem fair to me. Plus, I never really knew how to talk with God or even really learned how to pray to him in difficult situations. I had no real relationship. He was my mom's God that I inherited as a child, but he was never really a God that I served. After a few months, my mom asked me to come home and I would refuse. One day for no good reason, my aunt told me to leave. That's how I wound up returning home.

It was hard to adjust. Eventually things got back to feeling normal. As I continue growing, I would keep myself involved in school activities. That was one of my escapes so I wouldn't have to go home. I was on the step team; the ladies gave me a lot of comfort even though they probably didn't realize it. My coach at the time became like a second mom and her husband like a dad to me.

It seemed like my own dad stopped physically abusing me. I thought to myself I'm finally living a somewhat normal life. But that was short lived. Things turned for the worse once again. My dad and I went head on about another misunderstanding. I had just turned 18 years old and celebrated my birthday at school with friends. Two days later, we had a homecoming game and I left a note on the fridge, letting my parents know I would be at the football game and would make it home by 9:00 pm. I went out with friends, but I couldn't stay because I started getting a headache. My good friend took me home and I made it home at 9:00 pm. At the same time, my dad was having a conversation with my mom. He had told my mom if I didn't make it in the house by 9:00 pm he was going to deal with me.

Once I got inside the house, I was getting ready to go to bed because homecoming dance was the next day and I had to get ready. My dad came out and told me to come to him. I thought to myself that he was going to show me the letter on the fridge only to see a broom go across my head. I was completely shocked and ran inside the room to complain to my mom that my dad hit me. My dad began to complain and talk badly about me. He unjustly accused me saying that I was doing drugs and other unseemly things. He had never seen the letter on the fridge. He took all the gifts that my friends gave me and threw them all in the garbage.

I was completely fed up with him. I was tired of trying so hard and it never being enough. With tears in my eyes, I told him all those things he accused me of were not true. Then I left home. I went and stayed over at my friend's place because at the time she lived in an apartment. When I explained to my friends what had taken place, they wanted me to call the police, but I refused. I thought to myself what would happen to my younger brothers? The word had spread quickly to all my family of what had happened to me. Everyone was sad about my situation. Still I was left with no place to go. My godmother took me in again.

I was so stressed. I started losing weight and my hair was falling off. But I continued to move forward in life. When I was living with my godmother, my cousin was going to church. She invited me to go along with her and I did. That's when my life completely changed forever. I remember sitting in the back of the church and the pastor started talking about salvation. He asked, "If anyone wants to accept Jesus Christ as their Lord and Savior to come up". I felt him calling me, but I also could not move. My feet were literally stuck on the ground. I finally felt a force push me and I was able to walk in front of the altar. I gave my life completely to the Lord. I felt free. This God that my mother served had finally became my God. I had so much excitement that fear immediately left me. Difficult things in my life, no longer felt difficult. It didn't even bother me. I began to grow to know this amazing God. Within a couple of months, I was kicked out of my godmother's house and back home I went.

I forgave my dad, but he didn't want to have anything to do with me. I was rejected by him, but I was accepted by my spiritual father in Heaven. That gave me strength. God walked with me through the rest of the months in high school. I had a good friend that had rededicated her life with God. We both walked with God and that spirit of loneliness left. I graduated from high school but my dad did not attend. However my Heavenly Father was there with me. I moved to New York for 3 years and God began to show me how much he loved me. I built an intimate relationship with him. I no longer feared God because of hell, but I feared him out of reverence and respect. When I prayed, He listened. I knew He heard me. My prayers were answered. He showed me time and time again how much he loved me. He was a gentle Father. My faith grew in him more and more. My heart desired him more each day. He continued to show himself real in the simple things in my life and in the difficult moments. When I graduated with my Associates of Arts degree, the Lord told me to go back home. I submitted myself to the Lord, even when it was hard.

Eventually God healed and restored my relationship with my natural father. Everything that I lost as a child with my dad I got to experience it as an adult. I was forever grateful.

When I look back at my life, I see the hand of the enemy trying to use my dad to destroy the purpose and the will that God had over my life. In Ephesians 6:12 it reads, For we wrestle not against flesh and blood, but against principalities, against the rulers of the darkness of this world, against spiritual wickedness in high places. The enemy wanted to use my dad as a tool to destroy me, but he failed. He attacked me in my body, and my emotions.

Because I was both physically and mentally abused I went into depression. I felt I had no reason to live. I thank God he had a bigger purpose for me. Jesus said in John 6 all which he hath given me I should lose nothing. My life belongs to God and the enemy surely lost this battle.

My father passed away 4 years ago, but before he left, we were able to reconcile. I loved him and I know he loved me. I thank God for that. I serve such a mighty God not because of what he has done for me but because of who He is. I've grown so much in my walk with God. If God was unable to do anything for me the blood of Jesus was more than enough. Because he has chosen to step into the hardest time in my life, my life forever belongs to him. He sits on the throne of my heart and rules as He desires.

Deuteronomy 30:19 I call heaven and earth to record this day against you, that I have set before you life and death, blessing and cursing: therefore, choose life, that both thou and thy seed may live. Every day, I make that decision to choose him.

The Father's Wound

Tony Winans, Detroit, MI

My dad left my mother when I was 9 years old. The last thing I remember on that day is he pulled a new bike out the trunk for me; a black and white BMX. Of course, I was beyond excited!

His addiction to drugs is what drew him away from us. As time went by, the distance between he and I grew.

I was 16 when he promised to pick me up (just me) so we could spend time together. I was so excited. Then I received a phone call with yet another excuse (as I had received so many in the past). Sitting in a chair in my mother's room, I asked her with tears racing down my face, "Why doesn't he want me?" That was the last straw. I gave up on even the thought of reconciliation. I decided that I hated him and my life would be better off without him in it.

My confidence and trust in male role models were practically nonexistent. I would even use him as a model of what *not to be*. I made up my mind that I would raise my son (whom I had at the age of 18) purely from the superior attitude that I would not be like my dad. Of course, I loved my son but the unforgiveness I carried toward my dad contaminated my approach to fatherhood. In hindsight I realized I had neglected my son in the same manner that I was neglected. The sins of the father had perpetuated themselves.

I was judgmental toward my dad but gave myself grace for the same infractions, assuming myself to be a better father because I had no drug addiction. This blinded me to the love that I neglected to offer my son. I was too focused on not being my dad. Which was pretty easy, but too low of a standard.

My eyes were first opened when I gave my life to God and accepted Jesus as my Lord and Savior. Then I was able to see that I needed to forgive my father not only for the purpose of being a good dad myself. But I needed to be free to love and receive love from Jesus; and I could not do that while carrying unforgiveness. I also needed to forgive my dad because God had already forgiven him. So who was I to hold this offense over his head.

When my son was 15 years old, he and I drove down to see my dad. I was able to share with him all of the pent-up frustration and anger I had during childhood. I was able to offer my dad forgiveness. My dad received my apology and apologized to me. He was in a completely different place in his life and was able to articulate the pain he felt in choosing drugs over his kids. I wasn't aware of the pain of his addiction.

God had delivered him from the drug addiction, and he was building on his newfound relationship with God. I was thankful that we were able to build despite the past. But I was blown away by the way God transformed my perception of my father. I went from hating him to loving him so much I wanted to be like him. We didn't talk often but when we did talk, he would tell me how pleased he was with me. That meant a lot to me.

My father passed September of 2017. I was blessed to be able to forgive him before his passing. The forgiveness that God graced me to give to my father while he was here is a gift that I still carry with me today. I can say that I am honored that he was my dad.

All of Me

Pamela Gary, Farmington Hills, MI

I am married to the love of my life Terence. We have been married for 21 years, we have three daughters, and seven grandkids, two jobs and a very nice home. God has showed His kindness to us.

I know it's all because He loves me in spite of myself. I remember buying my first home, getting married, and opening my heart to two bonus daughters. However just one year later, I was lonely, unhappy, and miserable. I was in search of something, but I wasn't sure what I was searching for.

I was smoking cigarettes even though my youngest daughter had asthma really bad. I was also smoking weed. I was trying to drink when I knew I was not "really" a drinker. I was cursing and being disrespectful to my husband. I was also unforgiving, holding on to things that my sister, mom, friends and family or husband may have done or said to me.

In my mind, I was a really good person; and people were just mistreating me. I was full of myself (pride); always ready to run because that's what I did when things got uncomfortable for me.

One day, my daughter came home from work and told me that she was invited to church, and she asked if I wanted to go. I said yes. But when Sunday came, she changed her mind about going. Something in me needed to go, so I went, not knowing anybody there. I walked in but I almost didn't stay. I sat in the back and hoped that nobody saw me. The worship came forth and then tithes & offering. I mentioned this, because for some reason it meant something to me that day. Then the word came forth on forgiveness, MY GOD, and something broke in me that day. I received salvation and I joined the church. My life has not been the same since. I went home and told my husband and daughter, (and my husband came to the Lord also). So the next Sunday, I went, and I kept going. My heart and mind began to change. I was able to hear what God was trying to say to me. I began to have peace that didn't make sense. I revealed to God about my smoking (LOL) after he revealed to me about the sin in my life. I asked him to help me to stop smoking because I had tried plenty of times on my own but always ran back.

I remember one Sunday I was at the altar, and someone was praying for me, and I heard the Lord say "You will not cross this mountain again." From that day forward, I have not smoked again. I know it was nobody, but God. I couldn't have done this in my own strength. I had tried for many years and was unable. But in that moment, my God, my LORD delivered me. Yes, I Thank Jesus! My testimony is not just about being free from smoking, but really, God also freed me from bitterness. That word on forgiveness is what broke something in me. It let me see all of the unforgiveness I had stored in my heart towards other people. It also helped me to see how far gone I was in sin and how far away I was from God.

Thank You Jesus for your word because that was just the beginning of my journey in that span of time. Not only did you deliver me from smoking, but you also healed my hard heart and begin to heal my marriage, and all my relationships. You healed all of me. For that I am grateful.

MARRIAGE HEALING
& RESTORATION

Grounds for Marriage

Oscar & Crystal Jones, Coconut Creek, Florida

When we first married neither of us really knew Christ. We had a form of godliness – attending church occasionally. And we had enough sense to pray when we were in trouble. But that was the extent of our interaction with God. He didn't know us and we didn't know Him.

To be honest, we were both too young and too immature for marriage. We hadn't learned how to put each other's needs ahead of the other. We were both selfish, and lacking in basic communication skills. Most of our days were spent arguing and locked in power struggles. We were headed for disaster. Thankfully, God interrupted our foolishness and by the end of the first year, we both had committed our lives to Him.

Even though God was the head of our lives, we still had a lot of growing to do. Marriage was just too hard. We navigated as best we could with no tools and no real support. Babies were born, bills were made, life was tough. The struggles were relentless. We were raising 5 children and trying to navigate jobs, financial troubles, in-laws, health, self-image, etc.

I was an overbearing wife. Because I didn't know any other type of wife to be. My husband was passive aggressive, resisting my bid for control. It was a recipe for disaster. Often I would tell my husband I didn't want to lead. I wanted him to lead. But he didn't want to lead, and he didn't want me to lead either. And so we followed the recipe and disaster came – it culminated in adultery.

The Lord revealed the adultery to me in a dream. It was my worst nightmare. The thing I feared the most had come upon me. When I confronted my husband about it, he confessed. As things would play out, I asked him to leave. My heart was broken in two. Our whole life seemed to come crashing down. I was so devastated I could barely function. I cried every single day. I tried not to let my toddlers and young children see my tears. Their daddy was gone, and they asked for him every day.

Everything seemed so surreal. It wasn't enough that I already struggled with my self-image, I was already battling with rejection, but now I was the type of woman who was cheated on. More rejection. I slipped lower.

After trying to figure out what we should do, we decided to call the divorce attorney. It wasn't what we wanted, but it was what we thought we were supposed to do. The person on the other end of the phone gave us a quote that the starting price was $800, and if we had children, it could be more. We had four. We didn't even have the $800. We certainly couldn't come up with more. That was a lot of money in those days. We decided divorce was too costly.

We ultimately decided to *try* to work it out. That would require a whole lot of growing up on both of our parts. After making our decision to stay together, we went on the journey that God beckoned us on. We *completely* surrendered to God, not really knowing where it would land us. I was new in my walk with Christ. But I told the Lord I would do *all* that He asked.

God did surgery on my hard heart and on my husband's heart. We both needed deliverance; he from lust and I from bitterness. It was the hardest trial we ever had to walk through. We studied the Word and listened to messages. We prayed and worked on ourselves.

God had a bigger plan of redemption for us. Not only would he heal us and deliver us, but He would hand us the assignment to go help others. It was challenging, but we did follow His instructions. It was a painful transformation. There were so many times we didn't like each other. But because of who God is, we remained in the process.

Today, I can say, it's been an incredible journey. I thank God for not allowing us to give up. He needed to break up our fallow ground and rebuild our foundation. It was a dreadfully painful process, but so worth it.

Today, my husband is my closest and best friend. Our marriage has been filled with both devastating lows and some intoxicating highs. We still have to face challenges, but we are now so much more mature and better for it. God has blessed our union, and we are operating as a dynamic team – a force to be reckoned with. We stand flat-footed against the enemy and not each other.

Our relationship is transformed from the place we started; I am now a submissive wife. My husband is a phenomenal leader. Best of all, we are both submitted to God and walking out our faith. Our marriage has been turned inside out. All because God had a plan. I'm so grateful.

Today, as we celebrate nearly 43 years of marriage, we travel the country and abroad helping other marriages get to the other side of their pain and to hold on for a lifetime. God is no respecter of persons. What He did for us, He is able to do for others. Invite Him in.

Twice I Do

Cleave Davis, Waterford, MI

In 1989, I ran into my high-school sweetheart. We began to talk again. We both had been married and divorced. We talked for about a year, and then we decided that we wanted to get married. But we really hadn't thought things through clearly. We really hadn't considered what it would mean to blend two families together. But we got married, anyway.

About a year later, the problems manifested. The stress of finances and trying to blend two families became too difficult. We talked and we didn't feel heard by each other. So the only option I thought that I had was to divorce her. At that time, I didn't know God or that He hated divorce, so I followed the way of culture, and I divorced her. I didn't know how hard divorce would be. That was the most painful thing I have ever been through. When the judge said the divorce was granted, I felt numb all over. I remember thinking, "What have I done?"

I moved out. But after about a month, we began to talk again. She ran into some pastors that she knew. They had just started a church. She asked me to go to church with her one Sunday. I went just so she would quit asking me. I didn't know how my life would change, but after my first visit to the church, I gave my life to the Lord. Shortly after that, we asked the pastors if they would counsel us so that we could get remarried, and they agreed.

During that process, the Lord began to show me myself, and I didn't like what I saw.

But we continued on, until we completed the counseling. And we remarried on Nov. 24, 2000. We stayed together until my darling wife went home to be with the Lord. And I don't regret one day marrying or remarrying her. I just wish I could've had more time with her. And I wish I could do it over again.

For any man or woman that wants to know how to love their spouse the right way should read Ephesians 5:25-28 and by the way, I still attend that same church she invited me to. I'm still a member after 24 years.

MIRACLES

A Heart-Shaped Promise

Aries Winans, Detroit, MI

I found out I was pregnant by my long-time boyfriend. "Just get an abortion," he said. "I have to go college and don't have time for kids." I was determined to raise the baby myself if I had to, but just a few weeks later, I miscarried.

One year later, I gave my life to Christ. I wanted nothing more than to please God and surrender my life and body completely to Him. This is important to note because before I accepted the Lord into my heart, I lived a very wild life. I allowed my body to be mishandled by men and women. I was very promiscuous.

At 18, with my heart full of joy and anticipation, I was ready to give my all to God. I told the Lord, that one thing that I wanted more than anything was to be able to have children once I was married. I felt like I failed at everything else concerning my body. That was all I had left to offer Him. This meant a great deal to me. I was determined to live single and

62

celibate until marriage because I wanted to know what it meant to love God and learn to be loved by Him. I knew I wouldn't be able to focus fully if I were in a relationship.

After 6 years of living single and sold out for God, things began to happen in my life that derailed my focus and I began to backslide. If I'm being honest, it didn't feel like backsliding. It felt like I just stopped running for Him and ran the other way at full speed. *Nonetheless, that time of backsliding lasted several years.*

Fast forward a few years later to 2009 when I was living with my fiancé. Long story short, I ended up pregnant. I remember being so angry. I went into the bathroom and cried on the floor while kicking the cabinets. Why the theatrics, you ask? It's because I was reminded of the one thing I wanted to offer God - kids in wedlock. I felt like a failure. After about an hour of crying, I came out of the bathroom and talked to my fiancé about it. A few days went pass and I began to become a little excited about it. I didn't know that just a few short weeks later, I would have my 2nd miscarriage. This was just months before we got married.

On April 17, 2010, we finally said "I do". By November of that same year, we were pregnant, again. This time, we shared the great news with our family. Soon after we announced this pregnancy to our family, we lost the baby. This time around, we were just devastated. Heartbroken, to say the least.

My husband had a son from a previous relationship. While marriage granted me an amazing bonus son and I was grateful for him, I still wanted a child with my husband. We began to think we would not be able to have a child together. After a long heart-to-heart talk regarding how the loss of our second child impacted us, we cried together. All of this happened, and we had only been married a few months.

One day, we sat our son down and asked him how he felt about having a little brother or sister. He expressed his desire for a little brother. So, as a family, we asked God to bless us with a baby boy and give us, all of us, the desire of our hearts. After losing 2 babies in a year, we were uncertain of the possibility of having babies. We didn't know what was wrong.

Depression consumed me. I didn't understand why I kept having miscarriages. We sought out a local OBGYN to help us find answers. The doctor concluded that due to the heart shape of my uterus and my weight, I would *never* be able to carry to full term. He gave me no hope. No answers. No suggestions. Just another devastating blow. Again, I just felt defeated. I was being told that my dreams of having a child might not ever be a reality.

I felt like I was sinking deeper into a hole of sadness. Just seeing pregnant women around me caused jealousy to rise up in my heart. At this point, I decided I would take it to the Lord in prayer because I didn't want to live in depression any longer.

In late summer of 2011, we attended a prophetic service at our church that changed the direction of our lives forever. This particular day, our guest pastors from a ministry in California were speaking. The Spirit of God began to flow in that place and suddenly, there was a shift. A call was made for everyone who wanted prayer for anything to get in line and the prophets would pray. I ran to get in line. When it was my turn, my request was prayer for one thing, but the prophet of the house, who was already near, came behind me and said, "She wants babies!"

She spoke the desire of my heart that I had left by the wayside for fear of being disappointed. The pastor called up my husband to stand with me and they began to intercede on our behalf. The guest pastor asked me how many children I wanted; I said I wanted 3. It was my desire to give birth to 3 children because by that time I had already miscarried 3 children.

We left that service with a new hope in God. We believed that the Lord could do what the doctors said could never be.

After a few months, I began to pray and ask the Lord to direct us to another OBGYN. I went on Google, typed in OBGYN near me and 3 showed up within seconds. I prayed over them, and the Lord directed me to the lady in the middle. I had never heard of her before. I hadn't read any reviews or recommendations. I went with what I believed the Lord said and proceeded to make an appointment. This doctor was kind, considerate, and most importantly, compassionate. We came to her with hopeful hearts, desperate to find answers as to what we could do to carry to term.

In the middle of what was referred to as a "million-dollar workup" (it wasn't literally a million dollars), we got pregnant! She was just as shocked as we were! We were all so excited! We called our pastors immediately to share the great news of what the Lord had done. They prayed with us and encouraged us to trust God all the way. Around 9 weeks into the pregnancy, we announced to everyone that we were expecting. Even though we were excited, we knew that we had to stay in a place of prayer and continuously trust God no matter what. We kept our overseers informed of every appointment and every report. Together, the 4 of us prayed over every detail. We praised God with every milestone and trimester passed. When we found out we were having a boy, we were through the roof excited and couldn't wait to tell Anthony that God answered his prayer! He would soon have a little brother!

Around week 24, we were informed that there was a possibility that our baby boy may have deformities and if we wanted to consider terminating the pregnancy, now would be the time. Prior to this, we declined all testing to determine if there would be illnesses or deformities. When the doctor gave us this news, we looked at each other in agreement and told her that we were **not** going to terminate. We will love this baby no matter what the outcome. We are going to trust God no matter what. The OB later shared with us that our faith truly inspired her.

On January 29, 2013, we gave birth to a healthy baby boy with *no* birth defects, *no* illnesses or deformities of any kind. Glory to God! This same OB delivered our next 2 children bringing our total to 4 incredible children. God has truly blessed us and we are grateful! Things that are impossible with men are possible with God!

Bad Blood Turned for Good

Cleaver Davis, Waterford, MI

In 2013, I was diagnosed with hemochromatosis. It is a blood disorder, where your body produces too much iron. In most people, the intestines absorb the right amount of iron, but for those of us with this condition, the body stores the iron in joints, heart, liver, skin, pancreas, and pituitary gland. If not properly dealt with, it can cause the organs to stop working. The thought of this really scared me.

The only way to treat it is by having a therapeutic phlebotomy. A therapeutic phlebotomy is when you go to the doctor's office, and they remove the extra red blood cells by drawing your blood. For me, this meant that I would have to go to the doctor every two to three months to give 1-2 pints of blood. It felt annoying at first.

One day I went into my doctor's office for them to take blood, and the nurse suggested that I go donate blood to the Red Cross. She explained that I would no longer have to pay the doctor, and as a bonus, I would be able to help people. So I started to donate blood and platelets to the Red Cross. The blood that I donate is currently being used to help cancer patients. Every time I give blood, it helps 2-3 people. Since 2017, my blood has been used to help over 200 cancer patients. Isn't amazing that God would allow me the privilege to help cancer patients in this way? My body makes enough iron for me and several others. What a change in perspective. I'm just glad that I can help myself by helping others.

In Genesis 50:20 it reads, "But as for you, you meant evil against me; but God meant it for good, in order to bring it about as it is this day, to save many people alive ." I believe that applies to me.

A Way Out of No Way

Sherri Bryant, West Bloomfield, MI

I was diagnosed with Mesothelioma which is a type of lung cancer. During this adventure, I have experienced many stages in my treatment.

Stage 1 was immunotherapy.

Stage 2 was chemotherapy.

Stage 3 was surgery.

During each stage, God showed himself strong on my behalf. Before stage 3 began, I noticed large veins begin to appear under the skin on my chest. I showed them to my doctor who then scheduled me for an immediate vein mapping scan.

To my surprise, the scan revealed that I had a complete blockage of the SVC-Superior Vena Cava vein that supplies blood to the heart. Scar tissue from the chemotherapy lodged on top of the SVC vein which restricted the blood flow by 98%

to my heart. This was another crisis for the Bryant family, but not for the Lord

I asked my doctor, *"How am I still alive?!"*

It seems based on the scans, my body had created new veins. That's right, new veins! These new veins re-routed the blood, creating a new path bypassing the blockage, and allowing blood to get to my heart.

The Lord has created our bodies to be amazing. I love Him so much. Even before I knew there was a problem, King Jesus was at work making a new way for me to have abundant life! He continues to make a way for me. I am excited to see what He will do in the future.

A Way Out of No Way

Against All Odds

Lakara White, Grand Rapids, MI

I found out I was pregnant after I decided to separate from my abusive husband. This pregnancy really tested my faith. Doctors told me that my baby would most likely not live once I delivered. If my baby was to have a chance, I would need to deliver him early.

As a believer, I leaned on God. I wanted my baby to live. I wanted him to be okay. The Holy Spirit told me to pray. The cardiologist told me that he had a heart defect. If by chance, he made it, he would need surgery. I was even gifted a bear with his heartbeat in it to feel close to him just in case the worse was to happen.

With so many negative reports, fear was starting to take over. I remember coming home after one of my appointments letting all the tears that I didn't want the doctor to see spill out over my Bible. I was asking God, "Why?" He simply told me to trust him and to pray after every negative report that I receive. So, I did just that.

About 4 weeks before I was due to deliver, I was told that without a doubt, my baby would have some severe disabilities and complications. The doctors told me that they would prepare themselves to have all medical staff needed from different medical teams on board and ready on the day of my delivery.

I went home and I prayed. God gave me so much peace. Finally, I was at peace during a storm, not because I used substances which I would have done previous to my walk with God. But I had peace because I trusted God. He said He would keep in perfect peace those whose minds are steadfast, because they trust in Him.

My C-section was 9 hrs. long. My baby Milo was born with something called ventriculomegaly. Due to this condition and the increase of fluid building up, he had to have brain surgery to place a shunt in his brain to help it drain. He has had several procedures.

God is so trustworthy. I now have a beautiful, smart, fast-moving, healthy baby boy. Despite the challenges he's faced, baby Milo is defying the odds. There are some things that he has to overcome but with the help of physical therapy and the power of prayer. I am confident he will. Doctors said he may not even make it out my belly, breathing. He is now 20 months old. Jesus, the Chief Physician gives life and He is truly faithful.

Miracles of a Praying Mama

Claudia Thomas Troy, Michigan

There are times in our life that God is in full control. Sometimes the outcome of our circumstances is completely out of our control that's when our Father steps in to navigate our lives in ways and measures we could never understand.

This is a living testimony and walking miracle of one of those times. Let me count the miracles.

Miracle #1 God told us what was going to happen.

It was 11:59 pm on a Saturday night. L was getting ready for church, like l normally do. I dressed for bed with my pj's on. As I was walking towards my bedroom and ready to jump in bed, the Holy Spirit said to me "I'm getting ready to take your son home to glory". My son David was only 19. By the way, l have three sons but somehow l knew in my spirit which

son he was talking about. I answered the Lord oh so quickly as
l fell to my knees and said, No Lord! Not my son. I begin to
pray.

The house phone rang, and my husband answered. l could hear
the conversation and then my husband ran to the bedroom and
stated, "David has been in a car accident, and he is at the
hospital they are waiting for us to get there".

I didn't know how serious the accident was, but l knew it was
bad. On the way to the car my husband yelled "No you won't
Satan! You will not take my son!"

We begin to call family and friends to pray for us and our son.
Thank God for a praying community around us. No questions
were asked, people just knew it was time to pray.

Miracle #2. My son made it thru the night

We got to the hospital; the doctor talked to us in the lobby. He
said David had been in a serious accident. The car hit a building
and he was thrown through the windshield and had a grand
mal seizure, which is a type of seizure that involves a loss of
consciousness and violent muscle contractions. He also had a
very large laceration on his face. The impact of the crash was

so severe, they had to rush him into surgery and they weren't sure if he would make it through the night.

Miracle #3 He surrounded us with prayer warriors

After hearing this news, my husband and 1 wanted to cry. I remember the staff asking us, did we want a chaplain to come pray with us? We both answered at the same time, "We are the chaplains!"

My family and friends came walking in the room all at once like mighty warriors ready and armed for warfare. We were so thankful for our village. They helped us through this test of faith. This was a long battle, and we needed their support.

David was unconscious for a long time. One night while praying to the Lord for my son, 1 remember saying "Lord 1 know my son is in heaven with you. You tell him that his Mommy said he's got to come back. He's got to come back!"

Miracle #4 Believing for the Impossible.

David was hospitalized for 35 days. During that time, he had several surgeries. He stayed in ICU for 10 days and was unconscious for 5 of those days.

Later, he was moved to a regular room still dealing with a lot of mental challenges. He could look at a clock but didn't know what time was. He could look at a Bible but couldn't read it. He had to learn to walk and eat again. He was on a liquid diet for another 3 months. He couldn't swallow solid foods. It took months to develop his reading skills. He couldn't drive a car for a year.

When he did come home, he couldn't sleep. he needed 24-hour monitoring and care. His lungs collapsed twice, but God healed him. With therapy and time he was fully restored. He had 20/20 vision in both of his eyes. This was indeed a miracle. God had restored our son through the most difficult recovery.

Miracle #5. God honors prayer

The day he came out of the coma. He looked at me and said, "Mom, why did you call me back? Why did you call me here to be with you." I was stunned because I had only shared that request with the Lord. But I responded, "You're needed here, Son."

Miracle #6 God's restoration power.

He has fully restored my son, David. He is married with a beautiful, sweet wife and two beautiful sons. Because of God's grace, he was able to finish college with a degree in Accounting. He currently works with a utility company as a lineman.

OVERCOMING ADDICTIONS

Breaking Chains:
Deliverance from Porn and Sports

Oscar Jones, Coconut Creek, FL

The addiction to pornography started when I was a teenager. I stumbled upon Playboy magazines that were in our house. That opened the door. I was fascinated with these porn magazines. And I got hooked. As I got older, porn became a stronghold. I also begin to watch it in movies and on videos., The spirit of lust had taken control of me. As time went by, I frequently visited peep shows. The thing about lust is, it's never satisfied. As a result, my desires became stronger. As I opened up to this lustful spirit, I was more prone to addiction. I became addicted to sports as well. I would watch several games at once, flipping channels to keep track of each. I would spend excessive amounts of time watching sports.

These addictions begin to drive me, and caused me to do things I would later regret. The sports addiction interfered with my worship of God. It was an idol that I put in front of God.

The spirit of lust caused me to be obsessed with pornography even though at that time I would not have thought I was addicted. But that's what it was. This addiction nearly cost me my marriage, Eventually, it when I committed adultery. I am grateful for the grace and the mercy of God. But because God is so good, He began to convict my heart concerning both issues. I was tired of being controlled by these spirits.

I enlisted a friend who became my accountability partner. I listened to sermons about my identity and my manhood. God took me on a cleansing journey. It involved me understanding who He had created me to be. This helped me to deal with and overcome the spirit of lust that was in my heart since boyhood. Learning who God created to me brought me a sense of strength and commitment.

The Lord showed me how I lacked boundaries in my life. One of the ways he had me to establish boundaries, he asked me to not watch sports *at all* for the space of three years. He helped me to stay focused. I dove into the word of God and immersed myself into prayer. It is a joy to see how far God has brought me. He delivered me and set me free from the idols of sports and pornography. I remain very watchful of these spirits to this day. To God be the glory.

Depending on Drugs to Depending on Jesus

Keith Grier, Eastpointe, MI

At the age of seventeen, I started using drugs and alcohol, pretty much it was recreational use of marijuana, beer, and wine. At the time, it just seemed like the cool thing to do. It started out being mostly on the weekends. At some point, I started using drugs more and more often.

Eventually, I graduated to using powdered cocaine. I was living the street life, hanging, and partying. I started drinking more. I joined a gang and was doing a lot of really dumb stuff. We were fighting and making really bad decisions that could have cost me my life.

At about age twenty, I curtailed my drinking and started thinking about building a better future for myself. So I joined the army in 1979. That was one of the best decisions I had ever made. At the time, it allowed me to temporarily escape the reckless lifestyle I was living.

In 1979, I got married to the love of my life. She was the love of my life. We used to hang out and smoke marijuana together. Of course, I didn't know anything about being a man, husband, or a father.

Infidelity hit my marriage while I was overseas, and I didn't know how to deal with it. I was crushed. It was devasting to know my wife had stepped out on me; and it was with someone I knew. We started arguing a lot and it would escalate to abuse at times.

As an act of revenge. II also went out on the marriage t was foolish, but it happened. My use of alcohol and drugs escalated. Needless to say the first couple of years in the military were rough (self-inflicted). My wife had to go to my commander because I was spiraling out of control. I was put on report a couple of times.

We later moved to Seattle, Washington. Things were still challenging. Our marriage was still rocky. We decided to separate. My wife moved back to Detroit with my daughter. I was devastated. I wanted my family back. I was in love with my wife and my daughter was the apple of my eye.

While I was on leave, I went to Detroit to try to win my family back. I was there a few weeks. My wife decided to join me on my second tour in Germany. My second baby girl was born. A year later, I left the military in 1985 with honors. All glory be to God.

But when I came home in 1985, I started using crack cocaine. I was introduced by a family member, and everything went downhill from there. My wife and I went through divorce.

I got caught up in the madness of the addiction. It was a horrible existence. It was degrading to be controlled by drugs. People lost respect for me. They whispered. And to be honest I lost respect for myself. It was quite humiliating. Drugs robbed me of everything.

I was still working while still strung out. I eventually moved in with my mom. But I got so low that I stole a television from my mother. That was when I realized I had hit rock bottom. I left my mother's house because I was ashamed.

I found myself homeless. I went to Mariner's shelter. I wasn't able to get in. I slept on a porch of a house under construction. I knew I didn't fit into this street life of drugs. The addicts even told me I didn't belong. They actually thought I was a police officer. I knew that put me in harm's way. I needed to do something different because it was dangerous for them to suspect me of being an officer.

I went to the COTS (Coalition of Temporary Shelter) and was able to get in. I lived there for a while. I was homeless, drug addicted, with nothing. We were all quite pitiful. We were always hungry. When they fed us, we were hoping to get seconds. Sometimes we did and sometimes we didn't.

In 1995, one Sunday morning the staff took us to a church service. I was so tired of my life. I went up to the altar and give my life Christ. I was broken, ashamed, hurt, and I wanted my life back. And I asked God to deliver me from my drug and alcohol use. I felt a big weight lift off of me. I found myself crying tears of joy. I felt God had answered me. The drug deliverance didn't happen overnight. It took time. But God is faithful.

I got a job working at a machine company. I would take the bus to get there. I was also helping my dad with his cleaning business. Eventually I was able to get my own apartment. I felt like my life was getting better. During that time, I was afraid to be around users. And I did relapse a couple of times. But my heart and mind were free.

Off and on I would go to church with my brother and his wife. I wanted God in my life. It probably took a full year to get completely clean. God placed me in a church that gives to the community and helps the homeless. That was something I asked God for. And the Lord led me to Greater Works Family Ministries. My journey hasn't been easy and yes, I've failed several times along the way. But God never fails. When you REPENT, you get to start over. Please hear me, the amount of time it takes is irrelevant. All that matters is that you get free in Christ Jesus. To God be the Glory!!!

Unseen Addict

Lakara White, Grand Rapids, MI

I was like many people that "know *of* God" but do not truly know his character and all His amazing attributes.

Growing up as a little girl, "every" Sunday we went to church, and we didn't just go to church just to go. We had to make sure we looked "fresh to death", which back then meant "wearing your Sunday's best".

I really enjoyed going to church. It was more of a social event for me. I wanted to be seen with the best outfit. I wanted to see what boys would be there. And I loved the fun church functions which included food and snacks. So, as you can imagine the Lord was nowhere in my heart. I assumed he should have been because I was in church every Sunday.

Interestingly, I always prayed at night. This was not something I was taught. I guess it was a safe place for me. I enjoyed having conversations with God. Even though I didn't quite understand Him or really know Him, I was always drawn to pray. I felt like He was listening. Little did I know the Lord was producing in me faith that would prepare me for the journey that would lead me to Him.

Six kids later, I found myself trying to navigate an unhealthy, dysfunctional marriage for all the 13 years my husband and I had been together. Even though I endured different forms of abuse and infidelity, my husband became my idol. Everything revolved around pleasing him regardless if it wasn't pleasing to the Lord. It took me down a destructive path. On top of that, I lost my child when he was only 3 years old. He was very sickly. All these things brought me to my knees, but not in desperation for the Father. I felt so low, unseen, and unloved. I didn't feel the Lord near me and my circumstances, so I wanted nothing to do with Him.

I chose alcohol, drugs, pornography and eating to help me cope. I would literally eat till my stomach was so full I couldn't move. I knew it was insane, but I couldn't stop. I felt out of control. I drank every night, afternoon, and morning. My excuse was that I was okay because somehow, I still managed to take care of my kids, so I must not have a problem.

My addiction to porn became such a stronghold. I can remember being at my work desk watching porn on my computer, just to get a quick fix. It was seriously like a drug. Unfortunately I thought stuff like that was normal. I assumed everyone watched it. I had no clue how evil it was and the stronghold it had on me.

I always considered myself a funny, bubbly person, but I became so mean spirited and had so much hate in my heart. You would have had to set me on fire before I forgave someone. Pride was something I stood on and had no shame about it. I went on like this for years until I started to get tired of myself.

The Lord grabbed hold of me in my brokenness and I yielded. I started walking with him. Little by little, day by day, God pruned me and pulled me from many things that I thought I could not live without. I learned what it looks like to pick up your cross and follow him. I know what faith really looks like.

The Lord in his kindness has brought me through many hard trials. Because my heart was in such a wicked place I didn't really get to see the beauty of God's hands on my circumstances like I do now. Through faith in God, I have overcome the addictions of pornography, alcohol, drugs, food and other idols. I prayed for the desire to give up my addictions and the Lord has completely taken the desires away. God has was also working on my heart for some time, breaking away the pride and unforgiveness.

God is faithful. He has done so much for me, and I know He will continue. I am still standing for my marriage after 2 years of separation. I am interceding for my husband's salvation in faith that he will come back to Christ. Jesus is the lover of soul and I give all glory to him.

TRIUMPHING OVER DEPRESSION & REJECTION

An Eye to See

Nikerson Bonhomme, Hollywood, Florida

I was shot in the eye with a paintball gun. It did cost me my left eye. This caused me to slip into depression for several years. I had chosen to experience life apart from God because I blamed Him for my dad being mentally sick along with my eldest sister getting sick at the age of fifteen.

We went to church more than normal families. I eventually grew tired and figured I'd take control of my own destiny. Although, I had over a 3.0 GPA, loved school, and started on the JV football team my freshman year, my after-school antics are really what cost me my eye.

At the start of my sophomore year, I jumped into a stolen car with a group of friends for a joyride on Halloween. My mother had already warned me to come home, because she felt it was not safe outside. While joyriding, another vehicle with a group of friends starts shooting paintballs at the car I was in. One of the paintballs passed by two of my friends before hitting me directly in the left eye. I touched my eye to try to clear things up to see, but it was completely black. I couldn't see at all. A migraine would follow the entire day.

When I got the news from the doctors that I might not be able to see again, my heart dropped. I totally gave up all hope. I had dreamed of playing football and had thought that it would be the vehicle God used to bless my family. Over the years, my heart began to grow colder and colder, I began thinking about death. I sank into a deeper depression. Every night I would drink until I passed out.

One night after a night of partying, my cousin, being the designated driver, drove himself home where he then gave me my car so that I could drive about five miles home. I drove for one mile before passing out on the wheel. As I began to wake up, I found myself driving on the opposite side of the road. I hit the median before stopping in front of a palm tree with only a bent rim and a flat tire. All I could think of was how lucky I was because I was not dead.

Shortly after driving my car off the median, I went to change my tire, but the carjack broke. While thoughts of leaving the car to avoid a DUI rushed through my head, a mechanic stopped and proceeded to change my tire using a huge shop jack. He never spoke or even wanted the money I offered. He only drove off and waved, leaving me with the thought that was a weird encounter. I drove off thinking how *lucky* I was, with no thought of God or His involvement in saving my life that night.

Later that week at work, a man walks up to me and asks me do I believe in God? I replied yes, but I do not go to church. He then proceeds to invite me to Calvery Chapel, and it is at that moment God brought back to my remembrance that I had gone to a friend's funeral three months prior at that exact same church. During the ceremony, I recalled the pastor stating that for some here it was time for change. I left having felt every word of that message was for me, but never changed.

God had showed me that I was alive because He had not yet given up on me. Things were so clear. I changed that day and have been walking with the Lord ever since I was nineteen. (It's interesting because of my reckless life I thought I would be dead by 19). But God is so kind and merciful. I'm 39 today! Every time I tell this story it reminds me how great God is; even when we do not choose Him.

No More Tears

Domini Baldwin, Westland, MI

Let me start by saying, I am 41 years old, and life has just hit me full circle. I grew up in the church, and my family, starting with my God-fearing, loving, grandmother, have always instilled in me the importance of having a relationship with God. My mother and biological father did this as well. Although they had instilled this in me, I didn't quite understand what it meant to have a relationship with God.

I have always been a sad, depressed person, even as a child. I have always lived life, but never quite felt like I was flourishing. Although I may have tried to push through, I had never felt complete joy and happiness.

There were a lot of different emotions that I was dealing with that stemmed from my childhood. When I was a child, I watched my father physically abuse my mother. Once he slapped her down in front of a kerosene heater. This was a traumatic visual for me. I didn't know how to process the emotions, so I stuffed them. Sadness followed me throughout my life.

I can remember as far back as being 6 years old and having feelings of deep despair. A child shouldn't know anything about being sad.

I didn't understand at the time, but everything I was experiencing was spiritual. My mother grew up in the church, and she knew that she had a strong calling on her life. So what happens when you have a calling on your life? The devil tries to steal it from you.

My mother had been through a lot in her life. Not only in her teens but as a young adult. She experienced years of abuse from her children's fathers, which left her hurt and broken. It manifested when it came to her motherhood. Because of all the abuse, it left my mom kind of cold and aloof. Although I knew my mother loved me, she wasn't able to quite show it in the best way, at that time in her life. It was hard for my mother to be affectionate, which in return impacted me negatively. I was left feeling rejected and alone.

My biological father had all types of dysfunctions. He was an abuser, womanizer, and not a protective father. This also impacted me deeply.

As a teenager, I was looking for love in all the wrong places, trying to be grown per se. I became very rebellious, and it was like I just couldn't help but search for the love that I felt I was missing.

The void was so deep in me, and it was almost like a drug, where you keep trying, and keep going back and back again, but your soul is never satisfied.

I became rebellious. It was a lot for my mother. She didn't quite know how to deal with it, so she sent me away. She sent me to live with my aunt Beverly in California. This is where I believe the spirit of rejection came in, because although my mother felt that she was doing what was best for me, it left me feeling rejected and unwanted.

Now that I am grown and a mother, I do understand that just because we are adults and parents that doesn't mean that we are healed, or that we go about handling situations in the right manner. Many times we simply just don't know what to do. We mess up when we don't consult God. See sometimes as parents we hurt our children unintentionally. As time has went on, I was living with this unintentional pain, and I didn't even really know it, but God has a way of revealing what's going on inside of us, so that He can heal you, and give you the victory.

Fast forward to 2009, although I still didn't know what I was feeling, my relationship with my mom was growing. She had rededicated her life to Christ, she went to counseling, and allowed the Lord to heal her from her past hurts. She would remind me that God was always with me, and encourage me to get a true relationship with God. This is the year (2009) that my mother became terminally ill. This is when the flood gates of emotions came to the surface, that I never realized I had.

I could hear God speaking to my soul that I needed to get things right with my mother, as well as my father. Because as upset as I was with mother, I was also angry with my father. The rejection that I wrestled with not only came from my mother, but also my father. He did not protect me the way that a father should have. I also had resentment towards my father for the things he put my mother through.

During this time in my life, my emotions were at an all-time high. I remembered everything that was instilled in me as a child, and I started praying more, and listening to God. I felt and knew that it was time to forgive, but I didn't quite know how to. I began asking God to show me how to truly forgive.

God began working on my heart, before my mother passed away. I spoke with her about the way that I been feeling, and although she couldn't say much, (because she was so sick), I knew that she was sorry and that she had done the best that she could at the time. I also let her know that I had forgiven her. My mom had become my very best friend, and even in the midst of her being terminally ill, she still tried to make sure that we knew that God is the only way to get through life. We hammered in us that getting a relationship with God was most important.

My mother passed away on June 16, 2010. After her passing, I knew it was time to have a talk with my dad. We talked about it all. I told him how I remembered the things that he did to my mom. He apologized, and just like that I chose to forgive him. It was only by the grace of God.

As time went on, although I had forgiven my parents, I still felt a void in my life, and this is where it came full circle for me. I told God that I wanted to be whole, and that I no longer wanted to be sad and feel despair. I wanted to feel joy and happiness, even in the hard times.

I believe that God was speaking to me all along, that all I needed was to seek Him, only him, and I would be healed. I made a decision that I wanted to be healed and free, and I surrendered my life completely over to God. I began seeking him, learning about him, and began learning how very much he loves me. I should have never felt unwanted and rejected, because with God's love, you feel complete and whole. He will never leave us nor forsake us even though we may feel alone. He is always there.

Please give God a try. He loves you and wants to change your life. To God be the glory.

Rejecting Rejection

―――――――――― ✦ ――――――――――

Karen Grier, Detroit Michigan

I struggled with a spirit of rejection nearly my whole life. It caused me to isolate myself from people in fear of being rejected by them. This was something I carried from my childhood into my adulthood.

I missed out on so many opportunities in life, because of rejection. I worked a job for 17 years and never went in the break room to sit down and have lunch with my coworkers, because of the fear of rejection. It controlled my life. I was standoffish, bitter, suspicious, critical, and easily offended.

Rejection is connected to jealousy and gossip. I would be jealous if someone spoke to others and did not speak to me. I didn't know why they didn't speak. Maybe they didn't see me. I didn't care. That just gave me a reason to gossip about them.

Rejection took me on a rollercoaster ride. I was an emotional wreck. Rejection is self-sabotage. I had abortions. I sold my body for money. I was so deeply wounded on the inside; I couldn't see what I was doing to myself.

As a result, I settled into toxic unhealthy relationships. I spent 10 years in an abusive relationship, believing it would get better. And at least "he cared". I was okay with being abused as long as I wasn't rejected. I couldn't see abuse as rejection. I wanted to feel accepted at any cost.

I left one toxic relationship and got into another. I refused to walk away from the last one and hoped things would change. But I didn't want to make the change. That relationship ended in death. My friend took sick on the sixth of the month and died on the 29th of that same month. My heart was broken.

I would reject people and relationships before they had a chance to reject me. It left me in a lonely place. Ultimately, I didn't like the person I was. Rejection revealed my insecurity. I was so unhappy with myself.

It's sad that I spent so much of my life searching for love and acceptance, when it was always available through a relationship with God.

I remember going to the hospital because my chest was hurting. The doctor took x-rays when they came back, he used the medical term to explain it as a wall build up and behind it was stress. When I got home, I sat on the side of the bed and looked in the mirror. I thought it was time for a change. A family member had been inviting me to church. I called him up and said I'm going to church with you on Sunday. My first day there I felt drawn to something, so I kept going back to church.

I knew I needed something different. So I surrendered my life to Christ. Life in Christ makes a big difference. St. John 10:10 TNT states, "The thief comes only in order to steal, kill, and destroy. I have come in order that you might have life — life in all its fullness". That thief was trying to destroy me, but thanks be to God that it didn't work. Jesus came so that I can have a life and life more abundantly.

Now I'm living my best life. It's not found in the car I drive, the house I live in, or the trips that I take. My happiness is found in the love of God. The peace I experience surpasses my own understanding. God is so good he brought me through. He brought me out, I'm a living testimony about what God can do. New life is flowing through my veins. Without Christ, I had no peace.

Philippians 4:7 KJV says,

7 And the peace of God, which passeth all understanding, shall keep your hearts and minds through Christ Jesus.

That promise is enough to keep me from looking back. I never knew real love until I got to know Jesus. God has brought me through so much.

God has changed my life in so many ways. God is everything the Bible says he is. He is a protector, a provider, a peacemaker, a waymaker. God is just good. Who wouldn't want to serve a God like this? Everything you need is found in Jesus. Won't you accept him as your personal Lord and Savior? Develop a relationship with him. I guarantee you your life will be totally changed for the better.

Church Hurt

Marie Arias, Tamarac, Florida

For as long as I can remember I've always been in church. I was born and raised in church. I was a preacher's kid. I've always felt at a young age that Jesus was pulling me to have an intimate relationship with Him, beyond just going to church. So at the age of 9 years old, I made a conscience decision to give my life to Jesus. My Sunday school teacher prayed with me.

At the age of 14 years, my family and I moved to the U.S. I struggled mentally for the first couple of years. Throughout that time, I became very angry and emotional, I battled insecurities, fears, and loneliness. The transition of being in a new country, attending a new school, building a relationship with my mother whom I had not seen since I was 2 years old, learning a new language, and making new friends among many other things took a toll on me. It also affected my relationship with God. I found myself in a depressed state and I pulled away from God.

However, by my third and fourth year in high school, things looked much brighter as God allowed me to develop a friendship which at the time would literally change my life. Through that friendship I was encouraged and motivated to pursue God on a new level. God matured me and exposed me to a side of Him that I had yet to encounter. That friend and I became zealous for the things of God and all we wanted was Jesus. I wanted to see people going to heaven because that's what mattered to God.

Nevertheless, many years later after high school I found myself in a place where I despised the church. I struggled to keep a positive view of the church. I saw flaws and hypocrisy in the church.

On top of experiencing church hurt, I realized that I had given into trying to fit in and doing all the religious things because that's what seemed right. But in the midst of it, I was losing the authentic me, the freed me, the me that Jesus bled and died for, the me that Jesus called before the foundation of the earth.

I left the church for almost 2 years, and I did not attend a single church service. I would still read my Bible and worship every now and then, but I wanted nothing to do with the church.

One day I was hanging out at this bar, having a drink and listening to this live band playing, when suddenly I had an out of body experience. God started showing me each person's soul in that building. I started looking around and I saw demons holding on to some people in the room as they were dancing. It was such a dark atmosphere, it felt like a dream. I started praying in the spirit right then and there for salvation for these people.

That experience changed me. It made me realize that God is who He is and exists outside of who we are. No matter where we go, we can never be too far away from God. He is not God because of what we do or don't do but He is Yahweh, He remains constant whether we are or not. Secondly, that experience helped me to have sympathy for the church and not be so harsh and criticize it. His love for us (the church) and the unsaved has no bounds. Though challenging at times, I am learning as a believer to make myself available and continue to yield to God's will for my life.

The Final Blessing

If you don't know the Lord in the forgiveness of your sins and feel a tugging at your heart, perhaps it's time that you surrender your life to the Lord. Maybe you found that you were like some of the authors. You go to church, or you know of God, but you don't really live for Him. Or perhaps you used to live for Him, but have strayed away. Jesus invites you to come to Him. There is no judgment. And no shame. Your sin is not too big or too heinous for Him. For all of us have sinned and fell short of His glory. His loving arms are outstretched…waiting on you.

I John 1:9 NKJV reads, If we confess our sins, He is faithful and just to forgive us our sins and to cleanse us from all unrighteousness.

Romans 10:9 NKJV says, that if you confess with your mouth the Lord Jesus and believe in your heart that God has raised Him from the dead, you will be saved.

It's that simple. There is no 12-step program to salvation. It really is about repenting of your sins, confessing Christ as Lord, and believing that He is who He says He is. He does the cleansing. We just make ourselves available.

Today, you can receive Him right where you are. Talk to Him from your heart. If you need help, use this simple prayer as a guide:

Heavenly Father, I call to you in the name of Your Son Jesus Christ. Your Word says, "Whosoever shall call on the name of the Lord shall be saved" (*Acts 2:21*). I believe Jesus died on the cross for my sins, that He was raised from the dead on the third day, and He's alive right now. I repent of my sins and surrender myself totally and completely to You. Lord Jesus, I am asking You to come into my heart. Live Your life in me and through me forever.

If you have prayed this prayer, your past has been erased! And all things have become new! Praise be to God, you are a member of the family of God. You are now a born-again believer!

Find a mature believer or a Christian church that you can connect with to help you grow in your walk with God.

Welcome to your new life!

Your Testimony

Tell your story about how God brought you out.

Title: _____

_____

_____

_____

_____

_____

_____

_____

_____

_____

_____